The Joy of Marriage

Inspiration and Encouragement for Couples

by Monica & Bill Dodds

Meadowbrook Press

Distributed by Simon & Schuster
New York

Library of Congress Cataloging-in-Publication Data
Dodds, Monica.
The joy of marriage : inspiration and encouragement for couples / by Monica and Bill Dodds.
    p.   cm.
   1.   Marriage—Miscellanea.   I.   Dodds, Bill.
   HQ734.D636   1994
   306.81—dc20
                                                        94–7059
                                                        CIP

ISBN 0-88166-211-9

Simon & Schuster Ordering # 0-671-894-587

Editor: Bruce Lansky
Managing Editor: Dale E. Howard
Editorial Research: Craig Hansen
Photo Editor: David Tobey
Production Manager: Amy Unger
Desktop Prepress Manager: Jon C. Wright
Cover Photography: Bill Gale

Copyright ©1994 by Monica and Bill Dodds

Published by Meadowbrook Press, 5451 Smetana Drive, Minnetonka, MN 55343

BOOK TRADE DISTRIBUTION by Simon & Schuster, a division of Simon and Schuster, Inc., 1230 Avenue of the Americas, New York, NY 10020.

03 02   15 14 13 12 11

Printed in the United States of America

Acknowledgments

We would like to thank the people who served on a reading panel for this book: Jim & Ruth Brinker, Cathy Broberg, Sonja Brown, Chris Bruce, Eileen Daily, Charles Ghigna, Connie Jordan Green, Mary Harris, Jo Kittinger, Sydnie Meltzer Kleinhenz, Todd & Kim Koehler, Barbara Merchant, Robin Michel, Lois Muehl, Ken & Karin Neuvirth, Rebecca Rehfeld, Robert Scotellaro, Sherry Shunfenthal, and Nancy Sweetland.

We would also like to thank the photographers who contributed material used in this book: pp. vi and 97 © 1994 by H. Armstrong Roberts; p. 7 © Rajak Ohanian/Rapho; p. 11 © 1993 Archie Lieberman; pp. 16, 47, 79, and 84 © Bob Willoughby 1994; pp. 22, 35, and 105 © Jim Whitmer; p. 28 "Forsyth 1984" © 1984 by Paul F. Gero; p. 40 © Southern Stock Photo Agency; p. 52 "Mother of Ten" © 1965 by Johnny B. Jenkins (deceased); p. 59 © 1981 Ulrike Welsch Photos/courtesy *The Boston Globe*; p. 67 © Chris Harvey/Tony Stone Images; p. 73 © Leo de Wys/J. Norman; p. 91 © Frank Siteman/The Picture Cube.

All photographs are copyrighted and used with permission.

Dedication

To our parents, who have shown us the joy of marriage:

Russ and Terry Faudree
Married April 12, 1944
and
John and Margaret Dodds
Married June 14, 1941

Introduction

The joy of marriage is more than happiness, more than companionship, more than security. The joy of marriage is sharing a love so deep, so personal, it is life-sustaining.

That doesn't mean this joy is invisible. It can be seen every day in thoughtful acts between a husband and wife. It touches their family and friends, their neighbors and coworkers.

The joy of marriage is an ageless treasure shared by a man and a woman whose love for one another has changed each of them, bettered each of them, made each of them more than either would be without the love of the other.

A happy marriage is rooted in love. Joy is its blossom.

Monica Dodds

Bill Dodds

Monica and Bill Dodds

Sometimes Cupid hits the bull's-eye.

Falling in love doesn't mean you're suddenly stupid. You just act that way.

If he's your prince, it doesn't matter if others think he's a frog.

Love doesn't always happen at first sight.
Or second. Or third.

❧

Love can happen in an instant
and last a lifetime.

❧

Love changes lives.

❧

People in love want what's best for each other.

Remember: part of your lover will always be a mystery.

If life is a jigsaw puzzle, falling in love is finding the four corners.

The size of the diamond is much less important than the love it represents.

A marriage license is really just a learner's permit.

No marriage ever failed because the flowers at the wedding weren't perfect.

Marriage is not for wimps.

It takes courage to hold hands, exchange
wedding vows, and tell the world,
"We love each other.
We want to be together forever."

Getting married is like planting a seed:
just a beginning.

※

How to be a happily married couple can never
really be taught, only learned.

※

It's a lot easier to fall in love
than to stay in love.

※

Marriage holds no guarantees.
If you want a guarantee, buy a toaster.

A second marriage can feel like
a second chance at life.

Marriage isn't a destination;
it's a journey.

Bad weather needn't spoil a honeymoon.

Every newlywed couple has promises
to keep . . . and things to do
before they sleep.

Honeymoons are wasted on newlyweds.
They'd be happy anywhere.

In-laws, like mine fields in a meadow, make married life interesting.

Newlyweds can keep the best of both families' holiday traditions and begin to create some of their own.

Share each other's joy; feel each other's pain.

❧

Lean on each other's strengths;
forgive each other's weaknesses.

❧

When all else fails, try kissing the owie.

❧

Daydream together.

&

Doing nothing together can beat doing
something alone.

&

Love is wanting to tell your spouse something
new you learned, something wonderful you saw.

&

A joyful marriage is a bit of
heaven on earth.

When you're married, the road less traveled doesn't have to be lonely.

It's easier to face the future when you're walking arm-in-arm.

No marriage is all sunshine, but
two people can share one umbrella
if they huddle close.

Spending money on your spouse can't
replace spending time with him or her.

Sometimes sharing a bowl of popcorn
in front of the TV is better than dinner
at the finest restaurant in town.

No couple ever slept well
the night after they bid on their first house.

≈

Love makes a house a home.

≈

Sharing the housework makes it easier
to share the love.

≈

If she cooks, you clean.
If she cleans, you cook.

A loving spouse can see the good in you
even when you can't.

At times your spouse knows you better
than you know yourself.

Sometimes a spouse is like an anchor, keeping you safe and secure. Sometimes a spouse is like a sail, moving you to wonderful new places.

When life feels like a roller coaster,
you just need someone to hold on to.

The best comforter isn't
a down-filled quilt.

Love is being willing to face risks to see your spouse's dreams come true.

❧

Spouses who put their partners first have marriages that last.

❧

It's reassuring to know your spouse has faith in you.

❧

Best friends make the best spouses.

Marriage takes commitment;
all good things do.

You keep a lifetime commitment
by keeping promises day by day.

Faithfulness is like a candle shining
in a window on a cold and windy night.

Trust can be shattered with one
thoughtless act.

The difference between love and infatuation is
that love lasts.
Infatuation is just a flash in the pants.

The idea of using a "seven-year itch" as an
excuse needs to be scratched.

Love is the lubricant that keeps a marriage
running smoothly.

❧

Loving is a way of life, not a list of duties.

❧

Taking care of yourself physically says, "I love
you and I want to be with you a long time."

❧

Marriage is a hug, a squeeze, and
a desire to please.

You can never get, or give, too many hugs.

Hug therapy really works.

You never outgrow your need
for hugs.

Have your picture taken together
at a four-for-a-dollar photo booth.

Take time to notice, again, the great smile
your spouse has.

A warm smile can melt an iceberg.

Leave a love poem on your spouse's voice mail.

Send your spouse a love letter from
"A Secret Admirer."

Slow dance in the kitchen
when you're feeling romantic.

No love song sounds silly
if it's being sung to you.

Crank up the volume and sing along
when the radio's playing "your" song.

Every generation has its own love songs,
but they always contain the same message:
you and me, now and forever.

Love is life's no-calorie sweetener.

There's nothing like a love note slipped
into a lunch bag to make a peanut-butter
sandwich taste great.

You don't need company to use the best china.

Some of the most romantic dinners need
only one box of Chinese food and
two pairs of chopsticks.

Macaroni and cheese by candlelight
can be romantic.

Marriage doesn't pay a salary, but it does come with some terrific benefits.

Love and lust are not mutually exclusive.

Good sex—even great sex—is not enough.

Successful couples are friends
as well as lovers.

Good sex has as much to do with giving
as it does with getting.

If you've been rubbing your spouse
the wrong way all day, apologize and start
rubbing the right way.

Try a little tenderness.

Develop a private code for asking,
"Are you in the mood for love?"

❧

If you don't have a pet name for your
honey, make one up.

❧

Sex joins two bodies;
love joins two souls.

Sometimes it's fun to dress up and go out.
Sometimes it's more fun to undress
and stay home.

Adam and Eve were doing fine until they
started worrying about what to wear.

Buy a sexy nightie, even though you
know it's just going to end up
on the floor.

The best Valentine's Day gift is
unwrapped in the bedroom . . .
by candlelight.

The first one into a cold bed deserves
a warm kiss.

Warm your feet before you climb into bed.

Snuggle up on cold nights.

You're never too old to play footsie.

Sometimes the massage is the message.

Get sleeping bags that zip together.

Children don't divide a couple's
love—they multiply it.

Love is getting up
in the middle of the night with the baby
when it isn't your turn.

There's nothing like sitting side-by-side
at a ball game, cheering for
your child's team.

One of the best things you can do for
your children is to treat your
spouse with respect.

🔖

One of life's greatest joys is discovering
your spouse in your child.

🔖

Tell your children the story of how you met.

Look through your wedding album together.

Show your children your wedding dress—but don't try it on!

The best way for you and your spouse
to guarantee some time without the kids is
to do the dinner dishes together.

❧

You deserve a break: plan a weekend
without the kids.

❧

Find a hideaway—and use it!

❧

Take a walk together after dinner.

❧

Call if you're going to be late.

There's never enough time for everything in life. Make time for each other.

Next Saturday night,
take your spouse out on a date.

Happy husbands and wives don't do everything together.

Everyone needs time alone.

Learn to respect each other's space.

Manners still matter.

❦

Love makes it a pleasure to say, "After you."

❦

"Please" and "thank you" really are
magic words.

❦

Encouragement works. Nagging doesn't.

Never criticize how a spouse drives, cooks,
or diapers the baby.

Criticism works best when it's preceded
by praise.

Married couples don't always agree.

Disagree without being disagreeable.

Every good spouse is a patient teacher
and a willing student.

An apology is often the best policy.

Next time, put the toilet seat back down.

Don't expect your spouse to look great
first thing in the morning.

Draw a heart on the bathroom mirror
with soap and put both of your
initials in it.

&

A good-bye kiss.
Don't leave home without it.

Stand at the window and wave good-bye,
even if your spouse is just driving
to the store.

Honk when you pass each other in your cars.

Just hearing your spouse's car pull up
in the driveway makes you smile.

Turn on the garage lights
when your spouse comes home after dark.

You don't really know your spouse until you've traveled together.

If you really want to show her you love her, stop at the next gas station and ask for directions.

Smooch in the car at a stoplight

Tell each other stories of when
you were young.

Remember Thy Anniversary!

On birthdays, make wishes come true.

Give flowers; get kisses.

Give kisses; get flowers.

Remember the three C's of marriage:
communication, consideration,
and caresses.

Caresses can speak louder than words.

Good listeners make good lovers.

You can't listen and talk at the same time.

A smart spouse knows when to speak from the head and when to speak from the heart.

Better to talk now than to yell later.

Hundreds of marriage manuals
have been written with the same message:
keep talking, keep listening.

No couple ever went to a marriage counselor
with the complaint,
"We talk to each other too much."

If you don't tell your spouse the truth,
who will?

The harsher the truth, the gentler you tell it.

The happiest spouses have mastered
the fine art of knowing when to shut up.

It feels so good to sit side by side,
touching, not needing to talk.

Holding hands isn't just for teenagers.

🐌

Never go too long without holding hands.

🐌

It's hard to fight when you're holding hands.

🐌

Couples in love send messages
without talking.

Sometimes you can sense what your spouse
will say before a word is spoken.

Resist the temptation to finish
your spouse's sentences.

Just like magic,
compliments produce smiles.

♪

Spouses who give compliments,
get compliments.

♪

Don't wait till Valentine's Day to say,
"I love you."

Don't wait till your spouse is all dressed up
to say, "Wow, you look great!"

Learn how to say "I love you"
in a foreign language.

Don't wait till bedtime to whisper
sweet little nothings.

If you like Italian and your spouse likes Mexican, order a taco pizza.

Love is letting your spouse have the last piece of pie.

If you're a morning person and your spouse is a night owl, meet for lunch.

If compromise were easy, electric blankets wouldn't have dual controls.

A good marriage is like a house: there's always some room that needs a little work.

Any successful marriage includes
two skilled negotiators.

Keeping score in a marriage is one way
to guarantee nobody wins.

"We can work it out" is the motto of every
couple who stays married.

Marriages, like gardens, need tending.

"I'm sorry" is another way to say "I love you."

Making up and making out look a lot alike.

One kiss is worth a thousand words.

Happy spouses know
that the "adjustment period" in a marriage can
take up to fifty years.

Happy spouses also know
when to get out of each other's way.

Remember: The course of true love is
full of obstacles.

It takes two to tangle.

Love shouldn't hurt,
but once in a while it might sting a bit.

Sacrifice is part of marriage.
Always has been; always will be.

Marriage is like harmony:
two sets of notes for the same song.

The great thing about being married a long time is falling in love with the same person again . . . and again . . . and again.

There's nothing like having a crush on your spouse.

Passion doesn't have to dwindle; it can deepen.

Laughter is the sound of love.

Laugh together often.

What's love got to do with it? Everything!

How do you love your spouse? Count the ways.

Never underestimate the power of
a woman in love.

Love doesn't color the way you see the world; it just helps you notice its beauty.

Loving one person has changed *your* world.

Winter, spring, summer, or fall—that's the perfect season to be in love.

Marriage is a marathon, not a sprint.

Think of the first ten years as an appetizer.

How you celebrate your anniversary is far less important than how you treat your spouse the rest of the year.

The best anniversary celebrations have
a guest list of two.

Celebrate the anniversary of your first date.

Celebrate your un-anniversary.

One of life's greatest pleasures is growing
old with someone you love.

Skin may wrinkle and hair turn gray,
but the smile of someone in love
is ageless.

Celebrating a silver anniversary helps you appreciate those who have gone for the gold.

A bride is never more beautiful than on her fiftieth wedding anniversary.

No gift can match what a golden-anniversary couple has already been given.

Many married couples do
live happily ever after. Their joy
touches everyone they meet.

❦

Also from Meadowbrook Press

✦ **52 Romantic Evenings**
Unlike other books that provide only a brief outline of ideas, this book provides everything a couple needs to know to create romantic evenings that will make their relationship come alive, with complete plans for a year's worth of romance-filled evenings, including where to go, what music to play, what to wear, eat, and drink, and more.

✦ **The Best Wedding Shower Book**
This revised edition offers valuable time-tested advice on how to plan and host the perfect wedding shower with great games, activities, decorations, gift ideas, and recipes.

✦ **The Joy of…Series**
Six treasuries of wise and warm advice for that special parent, grandparent, spouse, sister, or friend in your life. These collections reflect the wittiest and wisest (and sometimes most amusing) sentiments ever written about those whom we hold most dear. Each book is illustrated with black and white photographs that poignantly depict the unique relationships between family and friends. These books are the perfect gift to show a loved one how much you care. *The Joy of Cats, Joy of Friendship, Joy of Grandparenting, Joy of Marriage, Joy of Parenthood*, and *Joy of Sisters*.

✦ **Our Bundle of Joy**
A celebration of birth, featuring poignant poems, quotes, and stories written by the world's best writers, wits, and poets. Makes a great baby-shower or new-baby gift.

**We offer many more titles written to delight, inform, and entertain.
To order books with a credit card or browse our full
selection of titles, visit our web site at:**

www.meadowbrookpress.com

or call toll-free to place an order, request a free catalog, or ask a question:

1-800-338-2232

Meadowbrook Press • 5451 Smetana Drive • Minnetonka, MN • 55343